It's a Tsunami!

by Nadia Higgins

illustrated by Damian Ward

Content Consultant: Steven A. Ackerman
Professor of Atmospheric Science
University of Wisconsin-Madison

visit us at www.abdopublishing.com

Published by Magic Wagon, a division of the ABDO Group, 8000 West 78th Street, Edina, Minnesota 55439. Copyright © 2010 by Abdo Consulting Group, Inc. International copyrights reserved in all countries. All rights reserved. No part of this book may be reproduced in any form without written permission from the publisher.

Looking Glass Library™ is a trademark and logo of Magic Wagon.

Printed in the United States of America, North Mankato, Minnesota.
092009
012010
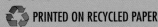 PRINTED ON RECYCLED PAPER

Text by Nadia Higgins
Illustrations by Damian Ward
Edited by Mari Kesselring
Interior layout and design by Nicole Brecke
Cover design by Becky Daum

Library of Congress Cataloging-in-Publication Data
Higgins, Nadia.
  It's a tsunami! / by Nadia Higgins ; illustrated by Damian Ward ; content consultant, Steven A. Ackerman.
       p. cm. — (Weather watchers)
  Includes index.
  ISBN 978-1-60270-731-3
  1. Tsunamis—Juvenile literature. I. Ward, Damian, 1977- ill. II. Title.
  GC221.5.H54 2010
  551.46'37—dc22
                                                      2009029376

Table of Contents

Warning Signs

The ocean sparkles. It is sunny and warm. People play along the beach. Then, strange things start happening.

Water on the shore starts heading out to sea. The ocean starts bubbling. Boats bob up and down like bath toys. A tsunami is coming!

Animals can
sense a tsunami
coming. Birds
stop making noise.
Crabs crawl out of
the ocean.

Disaster!

A tsunami is a giant sea wave. It spreads far over the beach. It can travel into towns. Then it slows down. It crashes back out to the sea.

Most tsunamis are about as tall as a telephone pole. A big tsunami could be as tall as a seven-story building.

The water picks up everything in its path. It can pick up cars, boats, and houses. More giant waves crash over the land. A tsunami can last for hours.

Help on the Way!

Rescue workers come to help. They look for missing people. They help those who are hurt. They clean up and build houses.

When a big tsunami hits, people around the world help out. Some people send money to buy food, blankets, and other supplies.

13

A Tsunami Begins

What causes a tsunami? A tsunami starts with a powerful earthquake. The earthquake shakes the ocean floor. It pushes up tons of water.

Almost all tsunamis are caused by earthquakes. But underwater volcanoes can cause one, too. When they erupt, they also push up tons of water.

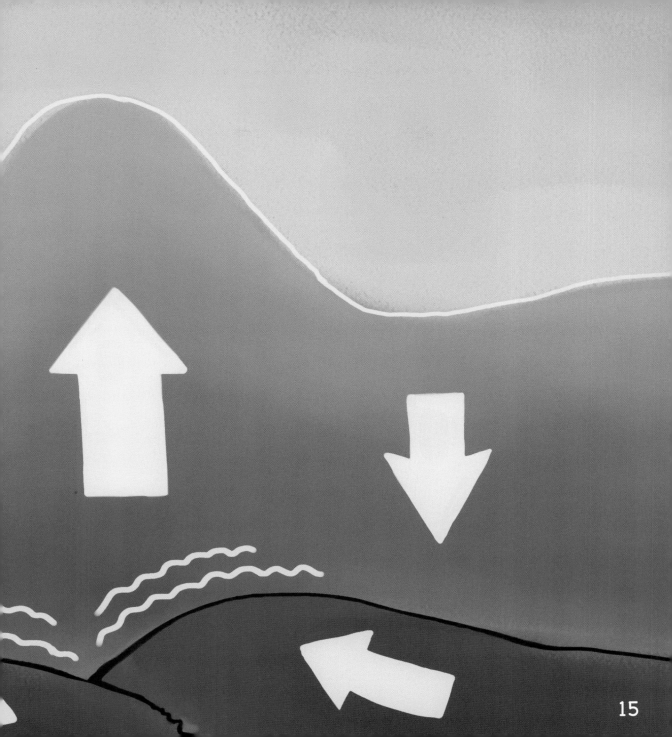

15

In the deep sea, the waves are small. You might not even notice a tsunami passing beneath your boat.

Big, flat waves start moving out in all directions. These waves can move as fast as airplanes.

The waves race toward shore. The bottoms of the waves drag along the ocean floor. They slow down. The water above piles up. The waves get taller until they slam onto the shore.

The Ring of Fire

Most tsunamis happen along the edges of the Pacific Ocean. This area is called the Ring of Fire.

North America

Pacific Ocean

South America

In the United States, Hawaii gets the most tsunamis—about one per year. Next is Alaska.

The West Coast of North America is in the Ring of Fire. In 1946, a deadly tsunami hit Hawaii. Nobody knew it was coming.

Later, scientists came up with a way to warn people about tsunamis. They started the Pacific Tsunami Warning Center.

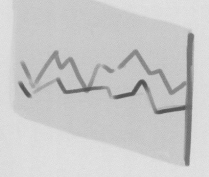

Tsunami Warning

Today, scientists can tell if an earthquake is happening in the Pacific Ocean. After an earthquake, there may be a tsunami warning.

There have been 20 tsunami warnings since the warning center began in 1949. Five of them were major tsunamis.

On December 26, 2004, the Indian Ocean produced a terrible tsunami. It hit many countries. Now there is a tsunami warning system for the Indian Ocean, too.

During a tsunami warning, people hurry to leave their homes. They go to higher ground. They stay there until the warning is over.

How a Tsunami Forms

1. An earthquake occurs in the ocean. It pushes water upward.

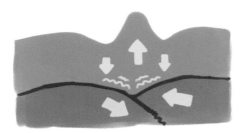

2. Waves created by the earthquake travel to the coast.

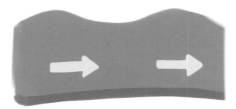

3. When the waves reach the coast, they become bigger. They smash against the shore and flood the land.

Tsunami Facts

Hardest Hit
Japan is an island country in eastern Asia. It is hit by more tsunamis than any other country.

Unusual Waves
Tsunami waves do not look like regular ocean waves. They are not curled over at the top, and they do not break. They look like a wall of water or like a rising flood.

A Fast Tsunami
In 2009, a strong underwater earthquake caused a powerful tsunami. The tsunami struck the small islands of American Samoa and Samoa near Australia. It hit so quickly that people had little time to run for higher ground.

Glossary

earthquake — a sudden shaking of the ground caused by movement in Earth's crust.

rescue — to save someone or something in danger.

Ring of Fire — a long, narrow, ring-shaped area around the edges of the Pacific Ocean where tsunamis are most likely to happen.

On the Web

To learn more about tsunamis, visit ABDO Group online at **www.abdopublishing.com**. Web sites about tsunamis are featured on our Book Links page. These links are routinely monitored and updated to provide the most current information available.

Index